*Quick*GUIDES
everything you need to know...fast

Relationship Fundraising

by Julian Smyth

reviewed by Morag and John Hocknull

WIREMILL
PUBLISHING LTD

Across the world the organizations and institutions that fundraise to finance their work are referred to in many different ways. They are charities, non-profits or not-for-profit organizations, non-governmental organizations (NGOs), voluntary organizations, academic institutions, agencies, etc. For ease of reading, we have used the term Nonprofit Organization, Organization or NPO as an umbrella term throughout the *Quick*Guide series. We have also used the spellings and punctuation used by the author.

Published by
Wiremill Publishing Ltd.
Edenbridge, Kent TN8 5PS, UK
info@wiremillpublishing.com
www.wiremillpublishing.com
www.quickguidesonline.com

British Library Cataloguing in Publication Data
A catalogue record for this book is available from the British Library.

ISBN Number 1-905053-16-9

Printed by Rhythm Consolidated Berhad, Malaysia
Cover Design by Jennie de Lima and Edward Way
Design by Colin Woodman Design

CONTENTS

RELATIONSHIP FUNDRAISING

INTRODUCTION

My father makes his donations to good causes once a year. It is always around Christmas, when he sits down and decides upon his philanthropic priorities, sending cheques to various charities and organisations. One of these is a major cancer charity. A few years ago, this charity began sending him solicitation packs and letters throughout the year, sometimes as often as once a month. He wrote to them and pointed out that he only gave once a year, so they could save their money on fancy letters and brochures by omitting him from their mailings. He heard nothing. The following year he wrote again – and again, nothing. Since then the amount of mail he receives from this charity has actually increased, and this year, such was his irritation, he decided not to donate at all.

This example of patently bad service from a nonprofit organisation to a donor is, unfortunately, not unique. It stems from a philosophy of fundraising which sees donors and prospective donors as "marks", unwilling victims of the fundraising department's wily schemes and devious stratagems. They are also the result of the high turnover in fundraising staff, which leads to a view that a dollar today is more useful than ten dollars tomorrow, even if this means that it is the only dollar the cause will ever receive from that particular donor.

Relationship fundraising is an antidote to this poison which threatens the income of all fundraising causes. In this book, we shall explore the reasons behind relationship fundraising as a method of generating voluntary income; the ways in which it can turn itinerant donors into lifelong friends of your organisation; and some of the tools of the trade you will need in order to put it into practice.

Reviewer's Comment

These comments are true the world over. The establishment of long-lasting and meaningful relationships between donors (be they current or potential) and the organisation seeking to acquire funds is the single most important aspect of successful fundraising. It is entirely possible that the representative of the organisation will never see the fruits of this relationship building, but the organisation certainly will.

WHAT IS RELATIONSHIP FUNDRAISING?

Relationship fundraising is simply answering the question "How would I like to be treated?" and dealing with one's supporters and donors in exactly that way.

In other words, think about the donor and the donor's agenda first, make your supporters friends and allies, and the money will flow. Treat them, above all, as individuals. No one likes to be sold to, no one likes to receive piles of junk mail, no one likes to be just a number – so why do so many organisations treat their donors that way?

It is also important to appreciate that marketing and fundraising are not the preserves solely of the marketing and fundraising departments. Every single employee, ancillary worker, trustee, volunteer and bottle washer is an integral part of showing a positive and caring face to the outside world. Fundraising is not, therefore, some bolt-on option which can exist separately from the cause itself; it must spring from within the organisation and reflect its values and concerns.

Keep the following truisms continually in your mind when planning and executing relationship fundraising strategies:

- People give to people.
- The main reason people do not give is because no one asks them.
- The person most likely to give is the one who gave last time.
- Fundraising is not about making money; it's about meeting needs and effecting change.
- Fundraising is not about making money; it's about making friends.
- No organisation has the right to public support; it has to be earned.
- A charity's real enemies are not other charities but distrust, uncertainty, fear of criticism, inertia, and confusion.
- Fundraising is what happens when everything else has gone right.

It is also important to understand why any of us might give to you or any charitable or nonprofit cause. These reasons often include:

- We want to feel good.
- We want be immortal.
- We want the world to be more like our own ideal.

Continues on next page

- We want to assuage our guilt in regard to a loved one or friend.

- We feel morally pressured to repay in a small way the many benefits we ourselves have received.

- We want to show off our wealth and be publicly praised.

- We want to join a club of our peers and thus benefit from the kudos which will accrue from being identified with them.

- We will do anything to avoid giving the government our money.

In other words, your cause may be a catalyst but not the primary reason for someone's donation.

It is important, therefore, not to become too idealistic when creating relationships with your supporters. Pragmatism is the key to real relationships, taking people as they are and forging mutually beneficial links that match the needs of your cause with the aspirations of your donors – whatever they are.

Here are some actual examples of current bad practice:

- An organisation which does not answer the phone at all, merely using an answering service.

- An institution which discourages all methods of donating except cheques because "it costs too much to administer".

- A medical charity which only accepts unrestricted donations.

- A charity which does not acknowledge gifts under a specific amount.

- An organisation which, as a matter of policy, does not ask its current donors for another gift until three years have elapsed so as "not to burden them".

- An educational establishment which only undertakes capital appeals, every eight or nine years, with no communication at all in between.

- A charity which "cleans" its database every three years and removes "lapsed" donors.

If these organisations had sat down and planned how to alienate their current and prospective supporters, they could not have done better than this. The relationship fundraising model requires a universal approach consisting of clarity, openness, honesty, friendliness, accessibility and vision: in other words, everything you would wish for from friends and family and that you have a right to expect from a cause to which you give money.

Reviewer's Comment
Relationship fundraising is a means of involving and informing people of your cause, and guiding them up the relationship ladder to become strong advocates of your fundraising programmes and message.

WHY YOU MUST HAVE A RELATIONAL DATABASE

A relationship depends upon what you know about the other person and the history of contact between you, which in turn informs the way in which you treat him or her. It is therefore vital that you have a method of storing this information in such a way that it is both retrievable and useful to you.

We are extraordinarily fortunate in this regard to be living in the age of the relational database – that is, a database in which every scrap of information can be related to every other scrap of information in order to link people together, segment according to a multitude of criteria, communicate, report, and analyse.

Your database is the single most important weapon in your fundraising armoury. It is a proactive marketing tool, not a computerised filing cabinet. It allows you to be creative and dynamic in your relationship-building programmes as well as keep a permanent record of the development of that relationship, of use not only to you now but also to anyone who may follow you.

What you hold in a relational database can be broken down into seven areas:

Biographical data – Who are the constituents? Where do they live? What methods of communication do you have with them? What is their marital status? Where do they work and for whom?

Relationship data – What are the connections of the constituents to you? Do they act as volunteers? Do they sit on any committees? If you are an educational or medical organisation, were they students and in what capacity?

Historical data – What is the background of your constituents? What have they done for you previously? Where did they work, study or live?

Interest-based data – What are their interests, hobbies, club or society memberships, giving patterns, involvement with other organisations?

Communications data – What have you sent the constituents? What have they sent you? This should include every telephone call, meeting, fax, email and letter, preferably with a direct link to the original document or note.

Link data – What links does any one record have with another? This can include outside interests, family relationships, friendships, internal committees and groupings, and employment.

Gift data – What have or are constituents giving to you? How have they donated – in response to which approach, which appeal, as part of which campaign?

The first thing to say about choosing a database is not to design your own. There is no substitute for the thousands of man-hours which have gone into the development of proprietary products and the hundreds of clients who have suggested improvements over the years. There are plenty of excellent systems on the market. Although they are by no means cheap, they will pay for themselves within a year or two with interest.

When sourcing a database, you need to assure yourself that it can deal with or supply the following areas:

Number of records – Can the system cope with the number of records you are likely to be placing within it?

Depth of information – As important as the number of records the system can hold is the amount, or depth, of information about each constituent. Can the system hold multiple address records, unlimited communication points, every possible salutation you might need to use, and current as well as past employment details?

Speed – Can it process your records quickly enough? Can you have someone's record up in front of you in the time it takes to say hello on the phone?

User-friendliness – Is it easy to learn and use by nontechnical people?

Flexibility – Can you adapt the system as you develop, adding new fields or changing formats with ease? What you think is totally

Continues on next page

adequate now may well not suffice in a few years' time.

Format – Does it integrate seamlessly with the mainstream products you are likely to be using alongside it? The most obvious of these is word-processing, but think also in terms of downloading financial data to spreadsheets and dynamic email and website links.

Service and support – Does the company supplying the product have an excellent support provision and automatic upgrades as part of a service contract? Always get your own references from current users.

Your database, once installed, then operates on three distinct levels:

- It allows you to interact with single records when in direct contact or when formulating a personal solicitation.

- It allows you to segment your database on literally infinite criteria. This can vastly improve the efficiency of your mailings and targeted approaches.

- It maintains your financial records, allowing you to report on your figures (and, where appropriate, make your tax claims), as well as ensure the proper stewardship of your donors.

Finally, having a database is not nearly enough if it is not kept up-to-date through constant care, thought and attention to detail.

Reviewer's Comment

The importance and relevance of successfully identifying donors through research and accurate data cannot be over-emphasised. Maintaining and keeping the database up-to-date is crucial to successful approaches. You must revisit the information you have added and ensure that it is current and relevant.

How would you like to be treated by your favourite nonprofit organisations, by those to whom you give support? Most people would say that they would like to feel appreciated, be kept informed and perhaps even consulted occasionally.

Personalisation of communications and an accurate and well-maintained database are clearly two of the most important elements to a friend-building exercise, but it is also useful to understand what it is that makes supporters committed to you. Ensure that you are giving them the information they need to assess your worth and your suitability for their support.

Check the following against your favourite organisation:

Issue – Do you care about what the organisation does? Are the group's concerns your concerns? Is the issue timely?

Credibility – Have you heard of the group? Does it strike you as well organised, competent and legitimate?

Referral – Do you know of this group through a friend, family member or colleague?

Enthusiasm – Do these people really care about their work? Can you sense their excitement?

Organisational history – What has the organisation done in the past? How do those accomplishments reflect its ability to get things done?

Realistic goals – If someone asked you for money to abolish stupidity, you would be pretty wary. If, on the other hand, someone wanted to abolish illiteracy, and had a reasonable plan to do it, you might give them a donation.

Uniqueness of organisation or project – Is the project filling a unique niche? Is the organisation trying to solve a new problem? Or does it have a new angle on an old problem?

Leadership – Who's running this thing, anyway?

Continues on next page

Constituency – Who will benefit if the group succeeds?

Networking – Will there be any new collaborations, new combinations of constituencies or interest groups?

Financial management – Can the organisation handle money in a professional way? Will it produce timely, accurate reports?

It is important to ensure that the individualism of donors is recognised and provision is made for it. How would your organisation fare in the following situations?

■ If a donor only wants communications to go via his office rather than his home, can you both amend his record accordingly and guarantee that his wish will be honoured?

■ If a donor only wishes to give at Christmas, can you ensure he is only asked at that time?

■ If he wishes to give anonymously, can you ensure his name does not appear on any list of donors you produce?

■ If he has seasonal addresses, can your systems adapt to mail him at the correct address dependent upon the time of year?

■ If he wants to donate on behalf of somebody else, or in memoriam, can you "soft credit" his gift so that both records show it?

Similarly, are you organisationally prepared to communicate with your donors? If they telephone, will anyone answer? If they leave a message, will anyone get back to them? If they write to you, how quickly (if at all) can they expect a reply? If what they say doesn't fit into a predetermined pigeonhole, does it get thrown away?

Reviewer's Comment
We have a favourite piece of music that we believe covers all aspects of relationship fundraising, and we suggest you try and obtain this and play it at your board meetings, volunteer information sessions, etc. It is "Taint What Ya Do It's The Way That Ya Do It" by Ella Fitzgerald. Most of the verses are relevant, but the chorus is the important few bars.

JUNK MAIL OR PERSONAL COMMUNICATIONS?

Since we need to keep in touch with our supporters, how then can we design our communications so that we are amongst those welcome contacts we look forward to rather than the junk mail and unwanted emails which clog our doorsteps and computers?

The answer remains the same as for all else in relationship fundraising – treat the supporter as an individual as far as possible. In this respect, content is much more important than packaging.

The most successful direct-mail campaigns on record are those that were carried out by the then Dr Barnardo's in the 1890s (a charity still in existence in the United Kingdom that looks after children). Hundreds of children were sat in large schoolrooms and made to copy, in beautiful copperplate, a letter written out on a blackboard. Personalised, hand-addressed and stamped, they were then sent out to all the charity's supporters. The response rate was magnificent.

What we must do is to attempt to come as close to this manual approach as is feasible. Try the following in order to achieve this:

- Review mailing lists for obvious errors before using them for unsolicited mail.

- Personalise your letters and emails in terms of the addressee and salutation and ensure these are correct.

- Don't write one letter to all of your constituents unless you can be sure it is relevant to all of them.

- Utilise as many different "field" options as you can in your letter, dragging in personal information from your database in order to make the letter as relevant as possible.

- If it is feasible, consider adding some personalisation by hand such as handwriting the salutation and/or signing the letters by hand.

- Use window envelopes rather than labels or print direct onto envelopes.

- Experiment with making your mailings as anonymous as possible on the outside. A reasonable-quality window envelope of standard size and shape could have anything inside it, so the recipient is almost certain to open it to find out what it is.

Continues on next page

- Keep your paragraphs short, the message clear and pithy, and try to keep the letter down to one page if at all possible.

- Keep the body of the letter simple and direct. Spend the money on the rest of the page (letterhead, quality of paper, message down the side, footer, etc.).

- Make sure it is as simple as possible for the recipient to respond to your mailing by including reply cards and prepaid envelopes. Also, make sure you have other ways of responding – websites, telephone numbers, email addresses – and list these in your communication.

- If using email, write it in plain text rather than HTML to ensure it gets past anti-spam software programmes.

The most important lesson to be learned about converting from junk mail to personal communications is not however, to be found in the mechanics of how you send your letters, packs and emails, but in what you send to people. If the only time your supporters hear from you is when you ask for money, then the relationship descends into that of a salesman with a customer, not a friend with a friend. A friend who is always sponging off you does not remain a friend for long.

Whilst, therefore, it is no bad thing to slip a response card and envelope into the back of an Annual Report that you send out, the letter that goes with it should not mention giving at all. You are communicating with your supporters, informing them of what has been happening with their money and their cause over the previous year – it is not necessarily the right time to be asking for money.

Reviewer's Comment
Being selective in the management of your communications and being discerning of the content and style of contact with your donors will ensure that the impression given is personal rather than automatic.

SAYING THANK YOU ... AND MEANING IT

You cannot say thank you enough. It is literally the first step in soliciting the next gift and is the only real reward a donor has a right to expect. The less personal the acknowledgement and thanks for a gift, the less appreciated the donor feels.

The following list contains just some of the ways one might consider thanking people and thus making the donation process that much more pleasurable:

- Make a quick telephone call just to say thank you when the gift arrives.

- Send a letter thanking the donor signed by a person and not a machine.

- Ensure that all mail and communications in future are personalised accurately.

- Send out a "welcome pack" spelling out how the gift will be utilised, giving further information about the work of the organisation, and showing how the donor can either become further involved or at least keep abreast of developments.

- Send an annual report or other materials produced by the organisation.

- Invite the donor to an open day to see the work of the organisation at close hand which is both practical (i.e. he/she can get to it) and feasible (i.e. it is not in two days' time).

- At the end of the financial year, send a note to the donor of the donations made to help him/her fill in his/her tax return.

- Make a note of the type of gift given and any preferences the donor may have signified concerning future gifts and then write to him/her with reference to these when asking for further support.

- Ensure the donor never again receives appeals via bought-in mailing lists as though he/she had never given before.

- Send the donor a Christmas card thanking him/her for his/her support over the previous year.

Continues on next page

Reviewer's Comment
Be mindful of the religious background of the recipient when sending a card with specific religious meaning. Receiving the wrong thing is worse than nothing.

What is important about all of these is the care and consideration that goes into them, the effort made to personalise and make relevant everything that subsequently is sent to a donor, and the relatively simple procedures required to put them all into place.

These are just as (one might even say more) important for a small organisation as for a larger one. Whether utilising large computer systems or simply doing things by hand, the process remains the same.

You should also consider thanking your donors in some material way – not one that costs you a great deal, but one which may mean a great deal to the donor. I have lost track of the number of certificates, plaques, scrolls, even fridge magnets I have seen in people's homes, offices and retail outlets. They must mean something if people are willing to frame them and stick them on the wall. This practice is also useful when growing your donors (see next page).

Reviewer's Comment
We have always recommended that "thank you" be said at least seven times for one gift. It is up to you to find the most meaningful seven "thank you" messages for your particular donors – letter, event invitation, phone call, personal contact, special lunch/breakfast/afternoon tea, a visit with the president/chair/principal of your organisation, etc. Other possibilities are inclusion on VIP invitation lists, small meaningful gifts, other family recognition options.

A carefully thought out and publicised thank you can also serve as a motivating factor for donors who are considering a donation.

GROWING YOUR DONORS

Knowing a great deal about your donors is not only useful in terms of maintaining accurate communications with them. It also allows you to "grow" them into more committed and generous supporters than they were heretofore. If you know their giving habits and what they prefer to support, you can tailor your requests to them so as to maximise their interest and, it is hoped, their generosity.

Remember that a new donor isn't simply a cheque or a pledge form. A donor is worth much more than simply what he or she will give you, vitally important though that is. He or she is also an advocate, a salesperson, and a volunteer. How you treat that person will determine how many of these additional roles he or she will fulfil for you.

An advocate – A happy donor will proclaim to all the world what a wonderful organisation you are, will defend you from attacks and slurs, will explain your position to third parties, and will promulgate your vision.

A salesperson – There is nothing like a contented donor to sell your organisation to others. Indeed, in some cultures, it is quite usual for one donor to press friends and relations to support his or her favourite cause (secure in the knowledge that he or she will, in turn, be asked to support theirs).

A volunteer – Volunteers are a fundraiser's lifeblood, whether manning stalls or undertaking major solicitations. Where better to find them than from your satisfied and enthusiastic donors?

It is extraordinary how many organisations run annual appeals for support with no reference back to their donors' giving histories. A standard appeal letter or pack is sent out as though it were the first time the donor had received anything from the organisation.

Again, using simple mail-merge techniques, you can personalise this approach to fit the history of the donor and, if you're lucky, increase the size of the gift.

Growing donors also means asking them to become more involved. Would they be willing to host a coffee morning? Could they see their way

Continues on next page

clear to taking part in a small survey of donors' opinions? Would they be willing to recommend your cause to their employer for matching funds? Would they be free on Saturday to take part in the annual flag day?

All of these requests are unlikely to be successful if you are seen as a total stranger. To friends, you will appear to be merely asking for a small favour.

Regular donors who understand what you are about, and feel informed and consulted will in due course respond to specific additional appeals, most commonly for capital projects that come about every few years.

Indeed, research suggests that those making the largest, most life-affirming gifts tend to have been contributing smaller regular gifts for between 11 and 13 years before making such a decision.

And, of course, there are bequests, about which more follows.

Reviewer's Comment
Adding value to the process of the relationship-building exercise is imperative to the overall success of any organisation's aims and objectives and the outcomes of any fundraising projects.

A bequest (a "gift on death" or "legacy", different words for the same thing) is a donor's ultimate gift. It signifies that the donor believes so passionately about your work that he or she would like that work to continue to flourish even beyond his or her own death. It is often the only time he or she can make a meaningful gift in terms of size. The majority of every nonprofit's database is full of those who are "cash-poor, asset-rich," and it is often only upon the realisation of the estate that such assets can be donated. In terms of relationship fundraising, therefore, the final manifestation of a lifelong relationship with you is to have left something for you in a Will.

In terms of value, legacies cannot be overestimated. Residuary legacies (wherein a donor leaves all or a proportion of the residue of the estate after specific bequests have been made) are ten times more valuable than pecuniary legacies (specific sums of money). Reversionary legacies (where the gift reverts to nonprofit once a surviving inheritor has had the benefit of it during his/her lifetime) are extremely popular with couples who wish to protect the remaining partner.

The development process often quoted whereby a donor reaches the point of making a bequest is as follows:

- Non-donor.
- Reactive donor (responding to an advert or a street collection).
- Single-gift direct donor.
- Regular donor (commitment over a number of years).
- Campaign donor (single larger gift for a specific purpose).
- Major donor.
- Legacy donor.

The problem with this approach is that it presupposes a donor's ability to make major, campaign, or even regular donations to you during his or her lifetime, and it is therefore all the more important to ensure that your relationship building and maintaining are not limited to those you believe capable of a major donation.

On the other side of the coin, however, it is equally important to realise that a legacy is an affirmation of a depth of feeling which does not arise from

Continues on next page

leaflets left in lawyers' waiting rooms or through small adverts in the national or regional press. As a result, most of the money set aside for legacy marketing is wasted as it is allocated primarily to advertising rather than communication.

If you have a meaningful relationship with your supporters, you can explain to them how important legacies are to you, how much they are valued and what they can achieve. You can ask them to consider leaving you a proportion of their estates and you can furnish them with useful information as to how to make a Will, what the different forms of legacy are, and how to write a codicil (an addition to a Will). You can recommend lawyers who will help them prepare their Wills, perhaps even at a reduced cost, and you can make it as easy as possible for them to let you know that they have taken your advice.

Perhaps the following would therefore be a useful checklist. Produce a legacy booklet which:

■ Explains the importance of writing a Will in general.

■ Explains the importance of bequests to you.

■ Explains different kinds of legacy.

■ Gives the correct wording to be used for each of the above.

■ Has a reply slip and a prepaid envelope for return.

Send it to those on your database over a predetermined age, along with a letter from another supporter who is leaving a legacy and is extolling the virtues of supporting in this way.

Think about suggesting a percentage of an estate that supporters might wish to consider leaving you – 1 percent or 2 percent is usual. Explain how much this could mean and that it is not only the wealthy who are able to make bequests.

If at all possible, ensure that every member of your board or council has made a Will naming you as a beneficiary and trumpet this fact in all your communications.

Plan on sending out your legacy brochure to all relevant constituents every year.

Unfortunately, for many organisations, this is as far as they go. As the completed legacy pledges come in to the office, they are entered into the records and a thank you letter is sent out. Then nothing. All the work that has gone into securing the legacy is put at risk by a lack of stewardship of these gifts that are just as real and probably more valuable than current donations.

You must maintain your donors' commitment for the rest of their lives or else another cause will nip in at the last minute and grab the bequest you have been confidently expecting.

Usually, some form of legacy society is created wherein members (all of whom have made a legacy pledge) receive personalised newsletters, advance information on events, and often an annual gathering (usually a lunch) where they can be thanked again and given personal briefings by the chair or chief executive.

Membership of such clubs or societies is publicly recognised at every opportunity and privately acknowledged with membership certificates, lapel badges, special ties and scarves, etc. It is in this way that the pledges are maintained. Unsurprisingly, there is also a marked increase in lifetime giving from such donors.

Reviewer's Comment
It is important to have a method by which donors will let you know they are interested in making a bequest, so you can maintain their interest and provide recognition and thank you opportunities even before the bequest is realised.

CONCLUSION

Relationship fundraising is not rocket science. It is, after all, common sense, isn't it? So why does it appear so hard to put into practice? There are a number of reasons:

Huge pressure is put on fundraisers by chief executives and boards to achieve results quickly, and this leads to quick-fix solutions which do not last. "Smash and grab" fundraising can solve a modest short-term problem, but heaven help you when the next problem surfaces.

Boards themselves fail to appreciate the importance of sustained investment and a long-term approach to donor development and they need to be educated. This is often where consultants can play their most useful role – not in terms of telling you anything new but in shouting the same message you have been trying to get across to your board with some authority.

The average tenure of development professionals is currently so short that it is natural not to invest much time and energy in a process for which the fundraiser will not see the benefit. That is also why legacy fundraising, which is so easy to do, is always the poor relation in most fundraising offices.

Outside direct-marketing firms, so-called face-to-face fundraisers, special-event teams and one-off grants organisers will continue to divert attention from the benefits of long-term donor development with their siren voices promising easy money. Many of them will indeed work in the short term, but every fad has its day and it is only direct donor involvement which will last. They should be seen as welcome additions, not substitutes for the core work of developing lifelong relationships with donors.

I hope that the common-sense, essentially human aspect of this approach will have convinced you of the merits of relationship fundraising, and that you will wish to ensure that your organisation joins the fortunate few who can honestly say that they have no customers, only friends.

CONCLUSION

Reviewer's Comment

Friend-raising and, therefore, relationship fundraising are like any exercise. Do the job well in the first place and it becomes easier as you become better at it and far more rewarding than you ever imagined.

For any campaign to work, a lead time of 18 months to two years is required to build worthwhile relationships. Training potential donors as well as volunteers and committee members is all part of the relationship fundraising process.

In a school or university, in particular, the "community" lasts a long time, therefore there is the need to identify ALL members of the community and nurture these friendships through informing and involving. Good stewardship of families from the day they start will bring successful results.

But all organisations have a community and good stewardship of the 'family' will bring successful results no matter what the organisation does or what services it provides or need it addresses.

JULIAN SMYTH, AUTHOR

Julian Smyth is the Principal Consultant of ASK Associates, a strategic fundraising consultancy based in the UK, and specialising in educational fundraising but with a number of mainstream charity clients.

Prior to becoming a consultant he was Director of Fundraising for the Royal Association for Deaf People, Development Director at Linacre College, Oxford, Director of the Bradfield Foundation and Director of the Sherborne School Foundation.

A passionate advocate of the relationship fundraising model, Julian is a regular speaker at conferences throughout the UK and Europe, was the founding chairman of the Independent Schools Development Forum, was on the founding executive committee of the Institute of Development Professionals in Education and edited its newsletter, was the first chair of the CASE Schools' Conference, and has written articles for *Professional Fundraising, the Journal of Non-profit Marketing*, CASE Currents and the IDPE.

Further details can be found at his website: www.ask.org.uk

Morag and John Hocknull, Reviewers

Morag and John Hocknull are both Fellows of the Association of Development & Alumni Professionals in Education Australasia Inc. (ADAPE) and full members of the Australian College of Educators (MACE). Morag is the first person specialising in fundraising for schools to graduate with a Business Certificate in Philanthropy and Nonprofit Studies at Queensland University of Technology and is the inaugural President of the Alumni association.

They have more than 35 years of experience in the Development/Advancement function. Their company, Education Development Office Management Service (EDOMS®), offers an advisory and mentoring service to boards, senior management and development office staff. They present regularly at conferences and workshops.

Their ultimate development office structure and philosophy is captured in their trademark "From Enrolment to Memorial" ®, and they have developed a software package, MATES ® (Managed Advancement Tracking Education System), that takes a school family through the relationship and fundraising process from enrolment (marketing function) to memorial (bequest function) and everything in between.

www.edoms.com.au